Catch the Wind

Softcover
ISBN 10: 1-59298-244-1
ISBN 13: 978-1-59298-244-8

Hardcover
ISBN 10: 1-59298-258-1
ISBN 13: 978-1-59298-258-5

Library of Congress Catalog Number: 2008932318
Printed in the United States of America
First Printing: 2008
12 11 10 09 08   5 4 3 2 1

Story by Anne Johnson
Illustrations by Shawn McCann
Cover and interior design by Ryan Scheife, Mayfly Design

Beaver's Pond Press, Inc.
7104 Ohms Lane, Suite 101
Edina, MN 55439-2129
(952) 829-8818
www.BeaversPondPress.com

To order, visit www.BookHouseFulfillment.com or call 1-800-901-3480. Reseller discounts available.

Mortenson | Renewable Energy Groups

Mortenson Construction would like to thank Beavers Pond Press and the design team for the hard work and seamless collaboration that went into producing this book.

10% Post-consumer waste

Fresh Ideas

If you've ever driven past a wind farm, you know that these towering machines have the power to stop you in your tracks or to at least compel you to take a second glance. If you have not had the experience of seeing a wind farm in person, your chances are improving. Wind energy is a rapidly growing renewable source of energy, and wind farms are sprouting up all across the United States.

Wind energy is part of the solution for a cleaner energy future. Wind power is homegrown energy; helping to lower home energy bills, create thousands of new jobs, and reduce the impact of global climate change. This book will introduce you to wind energy and give you an idea of what it takes to build a wind farm.

Knowledge is power, so seize the opportunity and learn how to catch the wind!

"I'm open!" Nels cried as he charged down the field. He saw his chance to score and booted the soccer ball toward the corner of the goal. Suddenly, the breeze that was blowing across the field became stronger. Nels felt a strong wind blow and begin to tug at his uniform. In one mighty gust, the wind blew the ball off course and away from the net.

Nels stood in shock as the referee's whistle signaled the end of the game. His kick was so powerful. How could the wind destroy his hopes of scoring for his team?

"What else has the wind destroyed?" Nels wondered. As he thought, he remembered photos he'd seen of swirling tornados, roofless buildings, and uprooted trees.

On the drive home, Nels sat in silence, upset over the wind ruining his chance to score.

"The power of mother nature is not always a bad thing," his father said. "The same wind that lifted your soccer ball away from the net can also provide **energy** to our home." Then Nels's father had an idea. "I think you should come to work with me tomorrow to explore the power of the wind. My construction company is working on an energy project called a **wind farm**."

"A wind farm?" Nels was confused so his father began to explain. "A farm produces food like meat, grain, or dairy products. That food is an energy source for our bodies. Just as a dairy farm produces milk, a wind farm produces energy. My company constructs wind **turbines** (tur-bins). They use the wind as an energy source and convert that energy into **electricity**. You could say that wind farms harvest wind energy." Nels was interested in learning more so he agreed to go to work with his father.

At home, Nels searched the Internet to learn about wind energy. He discovered that wind power begins with the sun. When the sun heats up an area of land, the air around that land absorbs some of the heat and becomes lighter. Colder air is heavier. As the warmer air rises, colder air moves in to take its place. This air movement is wind.

Did You Know?

To understand the air movement that creates wind, think of a hot air balloon. Air is heated by a gas flame below the balloon. The hot air rises into the balloon. The balloon fills up since the hot air inside is lighter, or less dense, than the cooler air outside the balloon. As the hot air rises, it carries the full balloon upward. When the gas flame is turned down, the air inside the balloon cools, and the balloon sinks back to the ground.

Because it is created and replenished naturally, wind is a renewable source of energy. Nels continued his search to explore energy and learned that there are two types: **renewable** and **non-renewable** energy.

What is NON-RENEWable Energy?

Non-renewable energy is energy from a resource that cannot be remade, or regrown, or is being used up faster than it can be made by nature. **Fossil fuels**, like oil, are non-renewable resources because they take millions of years to form and are in danger of being used up. People are consuming oil reserves at a faster rate than new supplies are being formed.

Natural Gas

Coal

Diesel

Gasoline

Think About It!

Oil, which is available only in limited amounts, is one example of non-renewable energy. Can you think of others?

What is RENEWable Energy?

Renewable energy is energy from a source that is naturally replenished, or renewed. Capturing wind energy is becoming more important as we look for **clean**, safe, and alternative resources for energy. Wind is a clean resource; wind farms produce no air or water pollution because no fuel is burned when energy is collected or converted to electricity.

Geothermal

Solar

Think About It!
What other renewable energy sources can you think of?

Wind

Water / Hydro

Nels had never visited a construction project site. He was so excited that he nearly forgot about the soccer game earlier that day. As he climbed into bed, he could hear the hum of the TV in the family room. He felt the heat warming him from the register near his bed. He saw the soft glow of the numbers on his alarm clock.

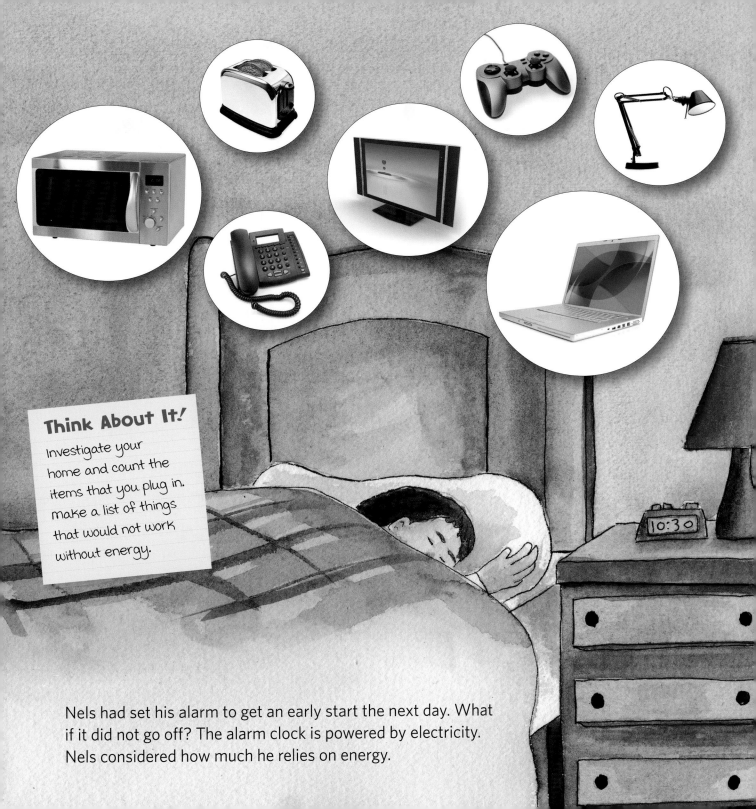

Think About It!

Investigate your home and count the items that you plug in. Make a list of things that would not work without energy.

Nels had set his alarm to get an early start the next day. What if it did not go off? The alarm clock is powered by electricity. Nels considered how much he relies on energy.

The next day, Nels and his father drove to the project site. As they drove, Nels noticed large towers scattered across the field. "The towers you see are wind turbines," his father explained. "The three blades on top are shaped to catch the wind. When they spin they turn a generator. The generator creates energy that is collected and sent to homes and businesses; in other words, wind turbines provide electricity."

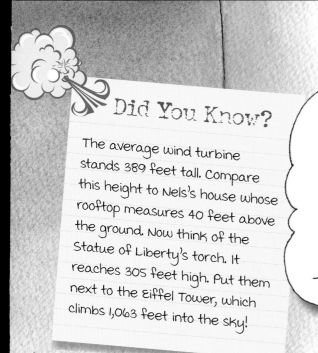

The turbines grew taller as Nels and his father approached. Finally, they pulled up to the site. As they walked toward the turbines, Nels felt as tiny as an ant. He could hardly believe it when his father told him that the structures stand taller than the Statue of Liberty. Nels watched the giant blades turning and remembered the soccer game and the gust of wind that blew his soccer ball off course.

Wind power has been used for centuries.

Kites

Nearly 2,800 years ago the kite was invented in China. The ancient Chinese used kites to measure distances, test the wind, signal, and communicate for military operations. A German company has developed ship-pulling kites as additional power sources for cargo ships.

Sailboats

A sailor manages the force of the wind, that fills the sails, to change the direction and speed of a sailboat. On a calm day, there is little wind energy available and the sailboat just drifts.

Ships

Using the combined forces of manpower and wind power, the trireme (try-reem) was a fast and agile ship. The ancient Greeks and Romans used them as warships. Teams of men rowed and sails were used for added power and to steer the ship on its course.

Windmills

In much of Europe, windmills grind grain or pump water. Millers attach large pieces of cloth to the blades. They can trim the cloth to change the speed of the rotation. Windmills were invented in Iran in the seventh century.

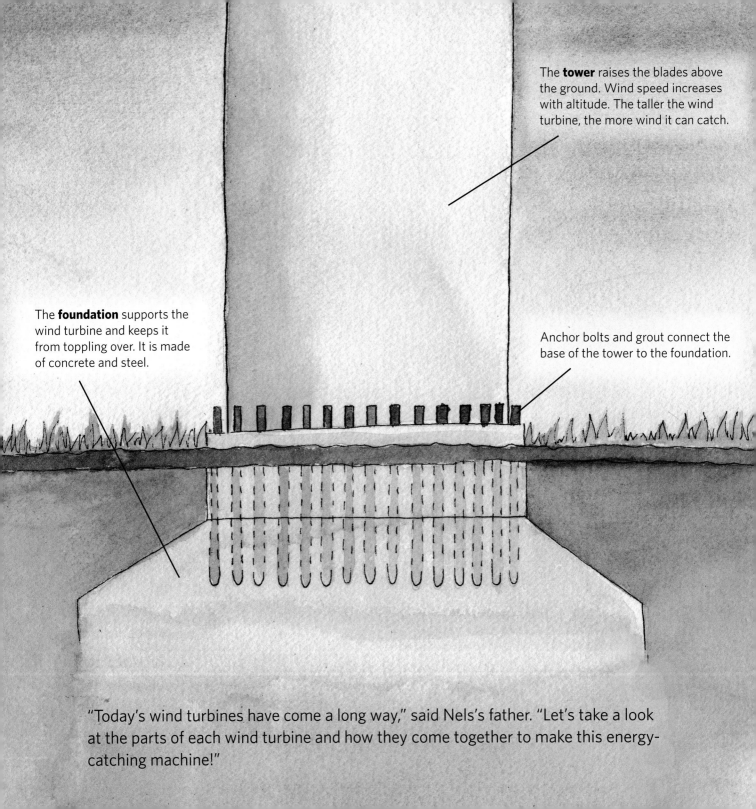

The **tower** raises the blades above the ground. Wind speed increases with altitude. The taller the wind turbine, the more wind it can catch.

The **foundation** supports the wind turbine and keeps it from toppling over. It is made of concrete and steel.

Anchor bolts and grout connect the base of the tower to the foundation.

"Today's wind turbines have come a long way," said Nels's father. "Let's take a look at the parts of each wind turbine and how they come together to make this energy-catching machine!"

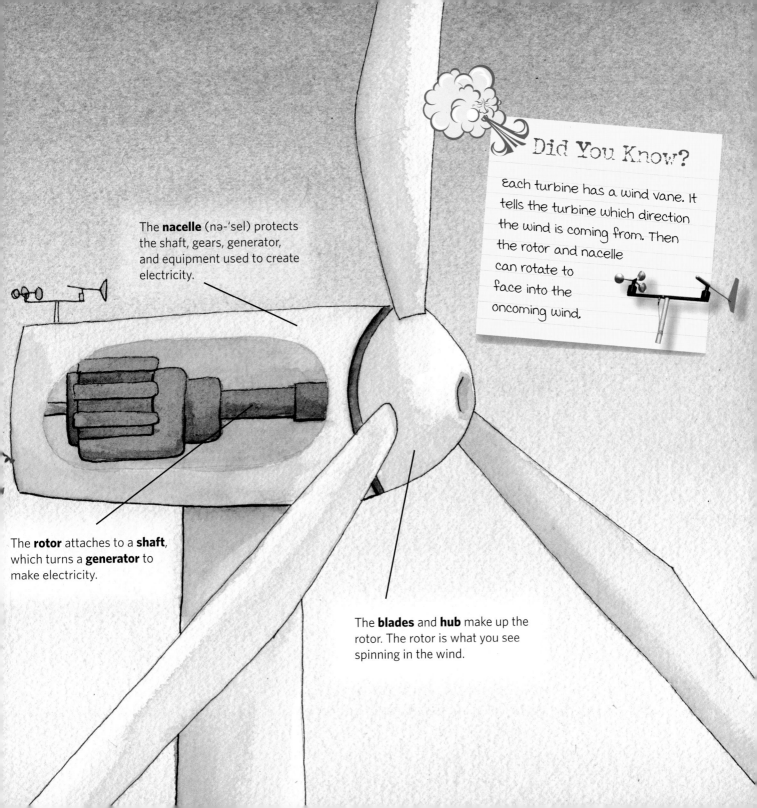

The **nacelle** (nə-'sel) protects the shaft, gears, generator, and equipment used to create electricity.

Did You Know?

Each turbine has a wind vane. It tells the turbine which direction the wind is coming from. Then the rotor and nacelle can rotate to face into the oncoming wind.

The **rotor** attaches to a **shaft**, which turns a **generator** to make electricity.

The **blades** and **hub** make up the rotor. The rotor is what you see spinning in the wind.

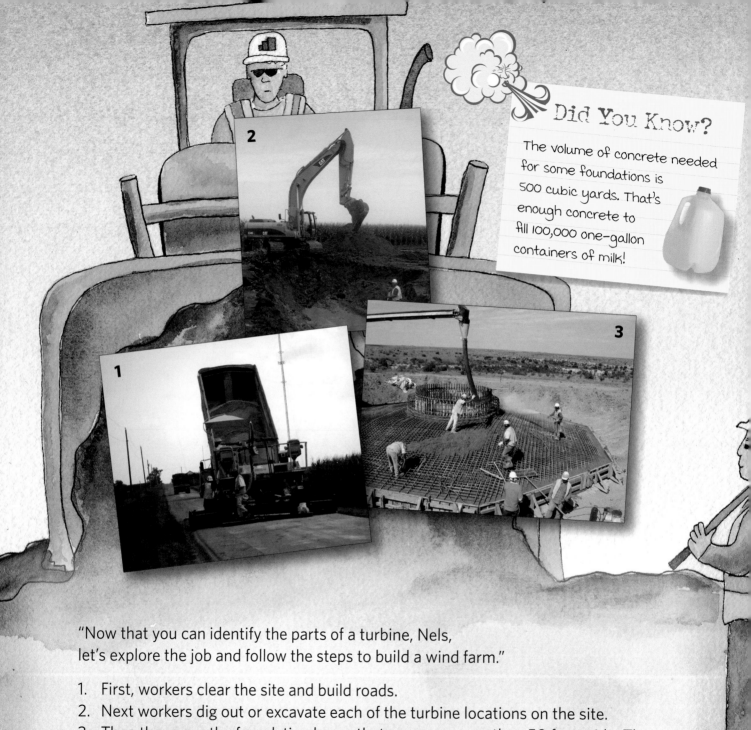

Did You Know?

The volume of concrete needed for some foundations is 500 cubic yards. That's enough concrete to fill 100,000 one-gallon containers of milk!

"Now that you can identify the parts of a turbine, Nels, let's explore the job and follow the steps to build a wind farm."

1. First, workers clear the site and build roads.
2. Next workers dig out or excavate each of the turbine locations on the site.
3. Then they pour the foundation bases that measure more than 50 feet wide. The turbine tower is bolted to the top of the foundation, called the pedestal.

4. Then cranes install the sections of the tower.
5. Some of the largest mobile cranes in the world are used to erect the towers and rotors. Sometimes the wind is too strong for the crane to work and it must wait to lift the pieces in place safely.
6. Bolts connect the base tower section to the foundation and each tower section to the next tower section.

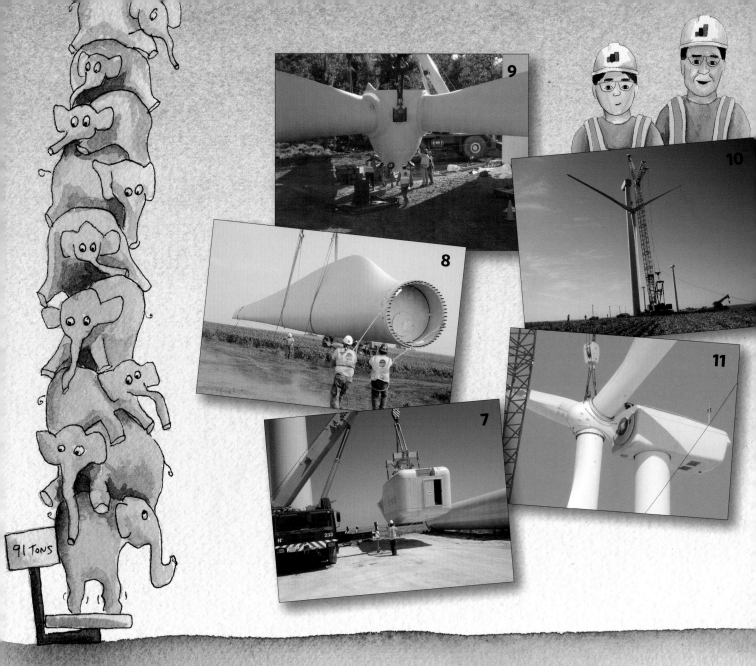

7. Then the cranes pick up the nacelle. It's the "brain" of the turbine, and can weigh up to 91 tons. That's equal to 16 elephants! It sits atop the tower 260 feet above the ground.

8. The blades for the turbine come to the site one at a time.

9. Workers attach the three blades to the hub on the ground to complete the rotor.

10-11. The crane lifts the rotor into place, and workers fasten it to the nacelle.

91 TONS

13

12

14

12-13. Once the turbine is up, workers wire the tower. Electricians climb up inside and run cables from the nacelle to the base of the turbine.

14. Workers bury electrical cables under the ground. The cables collect the electricity made by the turbines.

SAFETY AREA REQUIREMENTS

ZERO INJURIES

- 100% Hard Hats
- 100% Eye Protection
- 100% Warm-up Stretching
- 100% Fall Protection
- 100% Safety Vests

SHORTS, SLEEVELESS SHIRTS, ATHLETIC SHOES ARE NOT PERMITTED

Mortenson
construction

DANGER

Keep Out!
High Voltage Inside

If any child or person is seen inside this property, please immediately contact the number below.

Climbing the turbines seemed dangerous to Nels. His father pointed out two very important parts of building a wind farm: safety and quality of work. "Project team members work hard to ensure each task is done correctly and safely. Workers handle heavy pieces of equipment and climb towers every day." Nels noticed that safety was a priority on the project site. In what ways are workers are being protected?

"Why is the wind farm being built here?" Nels asked. His father explained that choosing the site to build a wind farm takes a lot of research. Scientists study the wind speed in an area to make sure it will be powerful enough and consistent enough to create energy. A site should have wind speeds of at least 11 to 13 mph. "That's about as fast as you can ride your bike!" his father said. After testing this farmland, scientists decided the conditions were perfect for a wind farm.

Some areas in the United States are windier than others. States in the Great Plains do not have mountains or too many trees to block the path of the wind. Flat farmland provides a great location for a wind farm.

According to the American Wind Energy Association (AWEA), the top five windiest states are North Dakota, Kansas, Texas, South Dakota, and Montana.

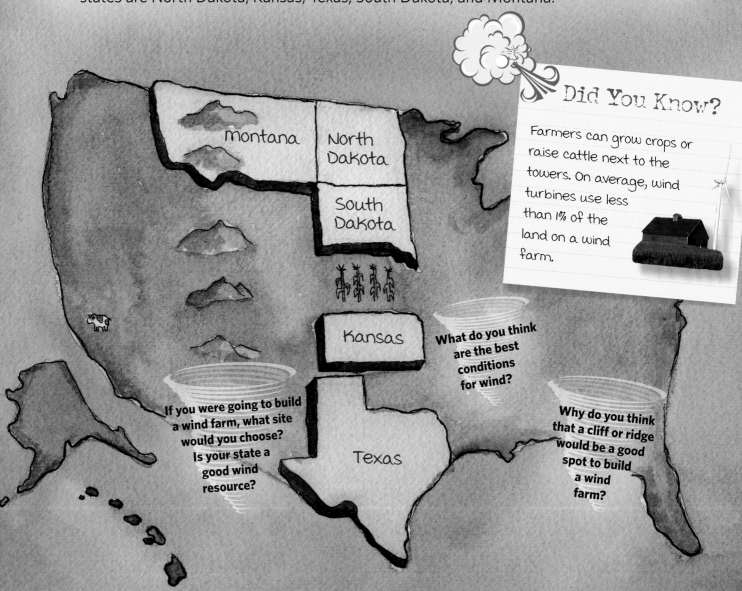

Did You Know?

Farmers can grow crops or raise cattle next to the towers. On average, wind turbines use less than 1% of the land on a wind farm.

What do you think are the best conditions for wind?

If you were going to build a wind farm, what site would you choose? Is your state a good wind resource?

Why do you think that a cliff or ridge would be a good spot to build a wind farm?

"In addition to benefiting the environment, wind farms benefit the communities where they are built by creating jobs," said Nels's father. "People are hired to manage the wind farm and to make sure the wind turbines are running correctly. Other jobs are also created because of the wind industry."

TRANSPORTATION companies ship the materials to the site. Sometimes parts for the wind turbines come from overseas!

ENVIRONMENTAL and **CIVIL ENGINEERS** make sure the site is suitable to build on and ensure the protection of native plants and animals.

LAWYERS help to put together contracts between landowners and wind farm developers.

CONSTRUCTION COMPANIES build the wind farms.

ENGINEERS design turbines, foundations, and electrical systems.

MANUFACTURERS produce the wind turbine parts.

"How does the electricity created by wind turbines get to our home?" Nels asked. The two met with the project electrical engineer, Alice, who helped them trace the energy's path through the site. Alice began with the blowing wind.

"When the wind blows, it rotates the blades of the turbine. The blades are attached to a shaft, which turns a generator in the nacelle. The generator creates electricity.

The electricity travels through cables running inside of the turbine, and out to a **transformer**," Alice continued.

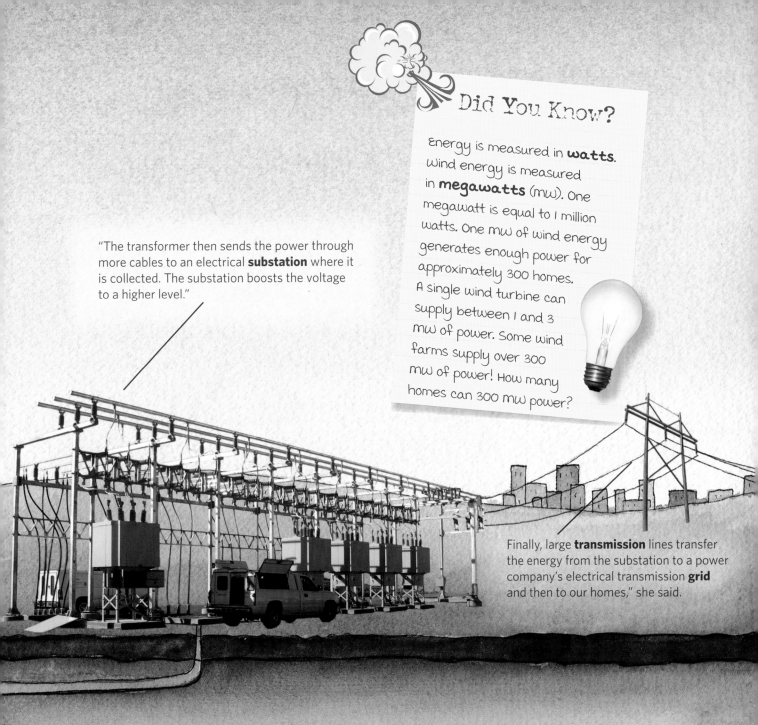

"The transformer then sends the power through more cables to an electrical **substation** where it is collected. The substation boosts the voltage to a higher level."

Finally, large **transmission** lines transfer the energy from the substation to a power company's electrical transmission **grid** and then to our homes," she said.

It made Nels feel good to know his father was building something that could power his community.

Nels wondered about people who don't have a wind farm in their community. Can they use wind power? Even if your electricity doesn't come from a wind farm, you can do your part in supporting wind energy by purchasing **renewable energy credits (REC)**.

Compare an energy credit to an orange. When customers buy oranges from the grocery store, more oranges need to be harvested to replace the stock. When stocks need to be replaced, farmers plant more orange trees to fill the orders. In the same way, when people buy wind energy in the form of a REC, more turbines need to be built to meet the demand. More wind turbines mean more clean energy!

DON'T FORGET
PENNIES
FOR
CREDIT
CHALLENGE

Think About It

What could your school do to purchase renewable energy credits (REC)? How many RECs would you have to purchase to power one home with clean energy for one year? How much energy does your school use each year? Can the energy used in a school year be offset with clean energy?

17,500 MW

15,000 MW

12,500 MW

10,000 MW

7,500 MW

5,000 MW

2,500 MW

1999

2002

2004

2006

2007

The wind power industry is growing! In 1999, 13 states supplied the United States with 2,500 MW of wind energy. By the end of 2007, that number jumped to 16,596 MW in 33 states! The United States has not yet reached its wind energy potential. Industry experts predict that, with proper development, wind energy could provide 20% of our nation's electrical energy needs. What will the future hold?

We use many resources to meet our energy demands. Non-renewable resources provide us with the most energy. To promote clean, renewable energy, the government has passed energy bills about how renewable energy, including wind, will supply our nation's electricity. The target is for a large portion of our nation's power to be supplied by renewable energy.

Electricity is measured in **kilowatt-hours** (kWh). A kilowatt-hour means 1 **kilowatt** (1,000 watts) of electricity is produced or used for 1 hour.

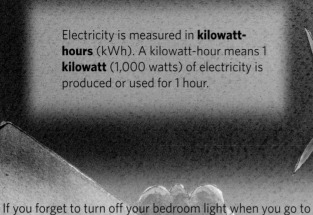

If you forget to turn off your bedroom light when you go to school, you are using up precious energy.

Energy = Power x Time.

One 50-watt light bulb left on for 20 hours consumes 1 kWh of electricity.

50 watts x 20 hours = 1,000 watt-hours = 1 kilowatt-hour.

Nels's household uses about 10,000 kWh each year. It would take the average 1 MW wind turbine a little more than 1 day to supply that much energy.

Using clean energy is important and it is just as important to conserve it.

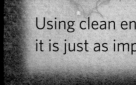

After learning about the power of wind, Nels was proud his father worked to build renewable energy. He wondered what other things he could do to help to save energy.

1. Turn off the lights when you leave the room.

2. Replace light bulbs with energy-efficient compact fluorescent light bulbs.

3. Turn off your computer screen when it is not being used.

4. Wait for a full load before you run the washing machine or dishwasher.

5. Open windows when the weather is nice to save cooling costs.

6. Add insulation to your attic to save heating costs.

7. Ride a bike, car pool, or ride the bus to conserve gasoline.

8. Recycle everything from pop cans to newspapers.

9. Don't let the faucet run while you brush your teeth.

10. Use a reusable water bottle instead of plastic bottles.

explore ways that you can make a difference each day!

Glossary

Anemometer - A device used to measure wind velocity as part of a wind resource assessment study. The anemometer typically is installed on a tower at the anticipated location and height of the potential wind turbine.

Blades - Most turbines have either two or three blades. Wind blowing over the blades causes the blades to "lift" and rotate.

Clean Energy - Energy, which does not pollute the atmosphere when used, as opposed to coal and oil, which do.

Controller - The controller starts up the turbine at wind speeds of about 8 to 16 miles per hour (mph) and shuts off the turbine at about 55 mph. Turbines do not operate at wind speeds above about 55 mph because they might be damaged by the high winds.

Electricity - The science dealing with electric charges and currents.

Energy – Any source of usable power, such as fossil fuel, electricity, or solar radiation.

Fossil Fuels - Any combustible material, such as oil, coal, or natural gas, derived from the remains of former life.

Foundation - The base below the surface of the ground on which the tower rests.

Generator - A machine that converts one form of energy into another.

Grid - A network of power lines or pipelines used to move energy from its source to consumers.

Hub – The central part of a rotor where the blades are inserted.

Kilowatt - A unit of electric demand, equal to 1,000 watts.

Kilowatt-Hour - A unit of energy equal to 1,000 watt-hours. It is a measure of electric energy generation or use.

Megawatt – Equal to 1,000 kilowatts or 1 million watts.

Meteorological (Met) Tower - A tower used at a project site that has equipment attached to it designed to measure wind resource. A met tower may have anemometers, wind direction vanes, temperature and pressure sensors, and other measurement devices attached to it at various levels above the ground.

Nacelle - The nacelle sits atop the tower and contains the gear box, low and high speed shafts, generator, and brake

Non-renewable Energy - Energy taken from finite resources such as fossil fuels.

Pitch - Blades are turned, or pitched, out of the wind to control the rotor speed and keep the rotor from turning in winds that are too high or too low to produce electricity.

Production Tax Credit - Provides the owner of a qualifying facility with an annual tax credit based on the amount of electricity generated.

Renewable Energy - Any naturally occurring, theoretically inexhaustible source of energy, not derived from fossil fuel, such as biomass, solar, wind, tidal, wave, and hydroelectric power.

Renewable Energy Credit - The "green" or renewable attribute of electricity that is generated through a renewable energy resource. A wind turbine that produces 1 MWh of electricity has produced 1 REC, which, in some electricity markets, can be sold separately from the electrical power.

Rotor - A rotating part of an electrical or mechanical device. The blades and the hub together are called the rotor.

Shaft - A rotating round, straight bar for transmitting motion and torque. It connects the rotor to the generator.

Substation - An auxiliary power station where electrical current is converted and voltage is stepped up or down.

Transformer - An electrical device by which alternating current of one voltage is changed to another voltage.

Transmission – The transfer of electric current from a power plant to a destination that could be hundreds of miles away.

Tower - Towers are made from tubular steel, concrete, or steel lattice. Because wind speed increases with height, taller towers enable turbines to capture more energy and generate more electricity.

Watt – The basic unit of electrical power.

Wind Farm – A large grouping of wind turbine generators located at a site having dependable strong winds.

Wind Turbine - A device for converting the flow of air into mechanical motion used to produce electricity.

Referenced Sources

American Wind Energy Association (AWEA)
U.S. Department of Energy, National Renewable Energy Lab
Windustry
U.S. Census Bureau

Websites on Wind Energy

To learn more about wind energy, visit these very informative websites!

Windustry
http://www.windustry.org

AWEA
http://www.awea.org

Department of Renewable Energy:
Energy Efficiency and Renewable Energy
http://www.eere.energy.gov/kids

Kidwind Project
http://www.kidwind.org

Community Energy
http://www.newwindenergy.com

National Energy Education Development Project, NEED
http://need.org/curriculum.php#WINDEC

Wind with Miller
http://www.windpower.org/en/kids/index.htm

Special Thanks

Mortenson would like to thank its project teams whose photographs appear throughout the book.